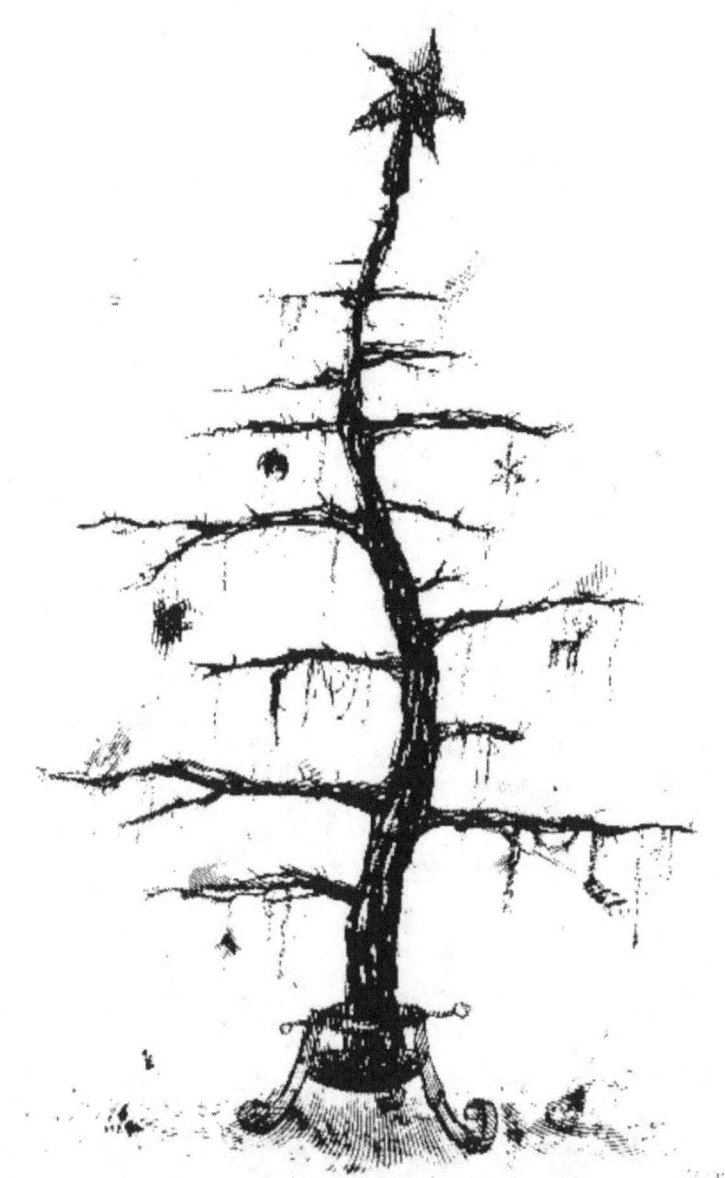

Adults
ANTI – CHRISTMAS
Colouring Book

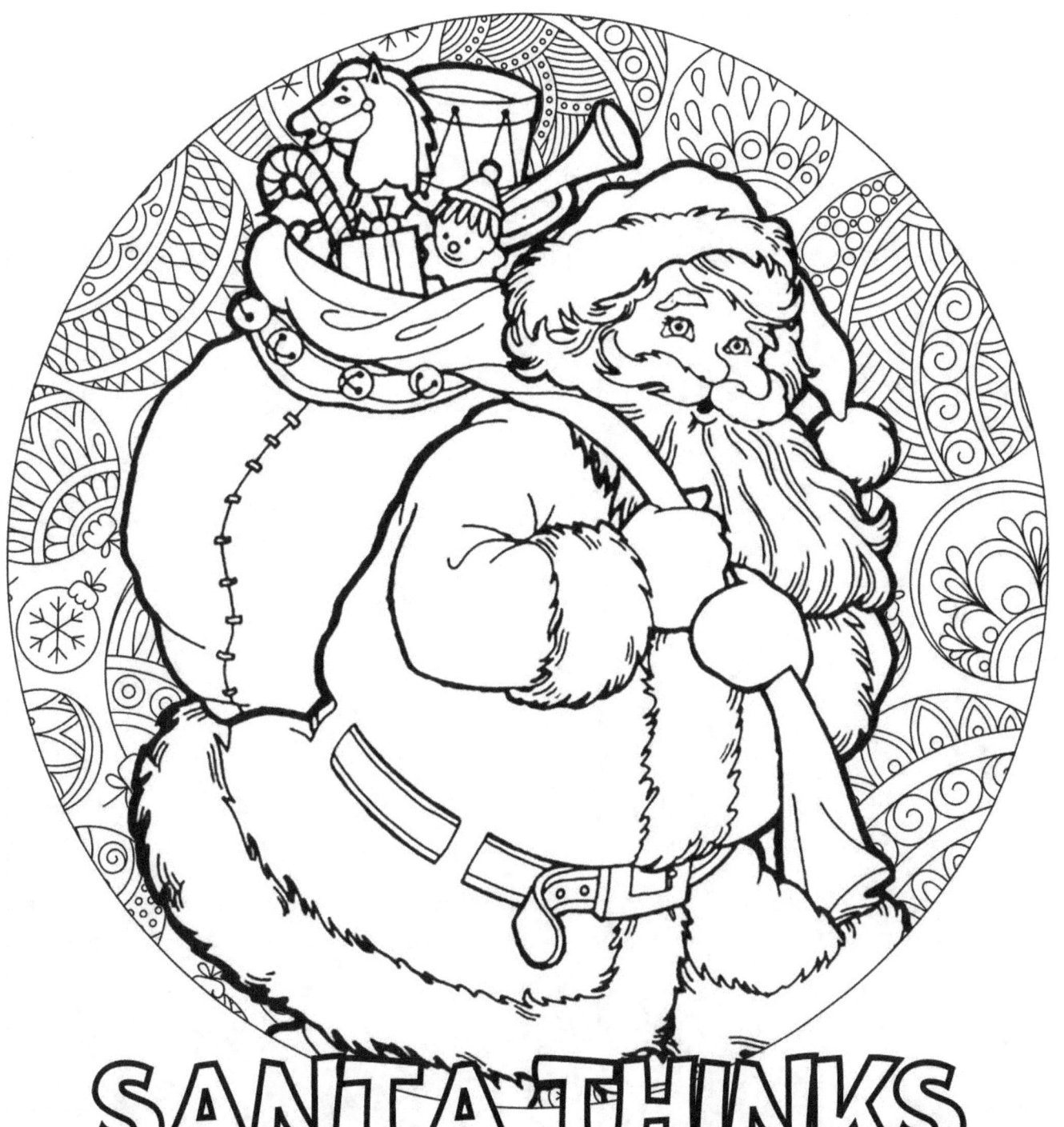

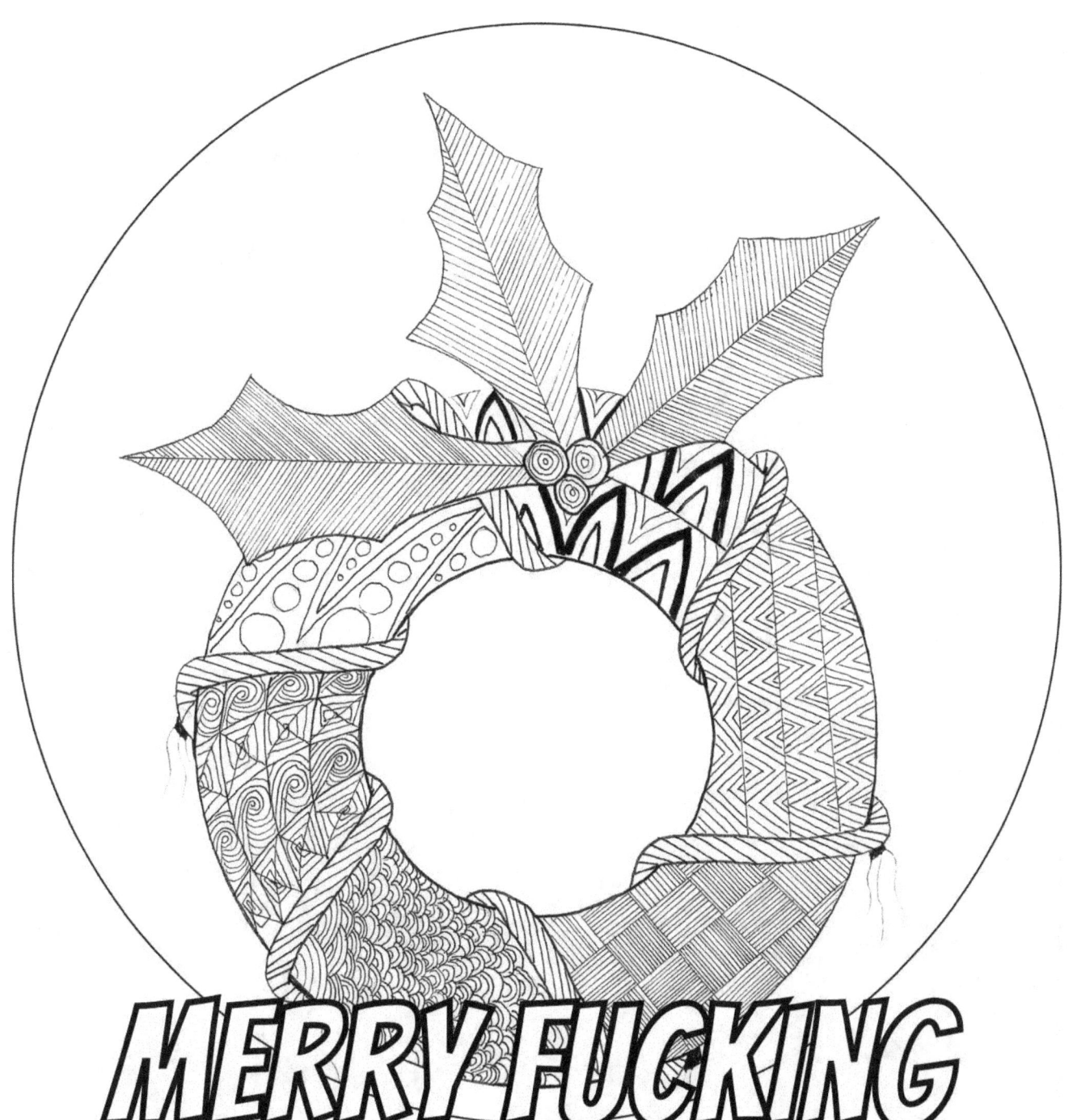

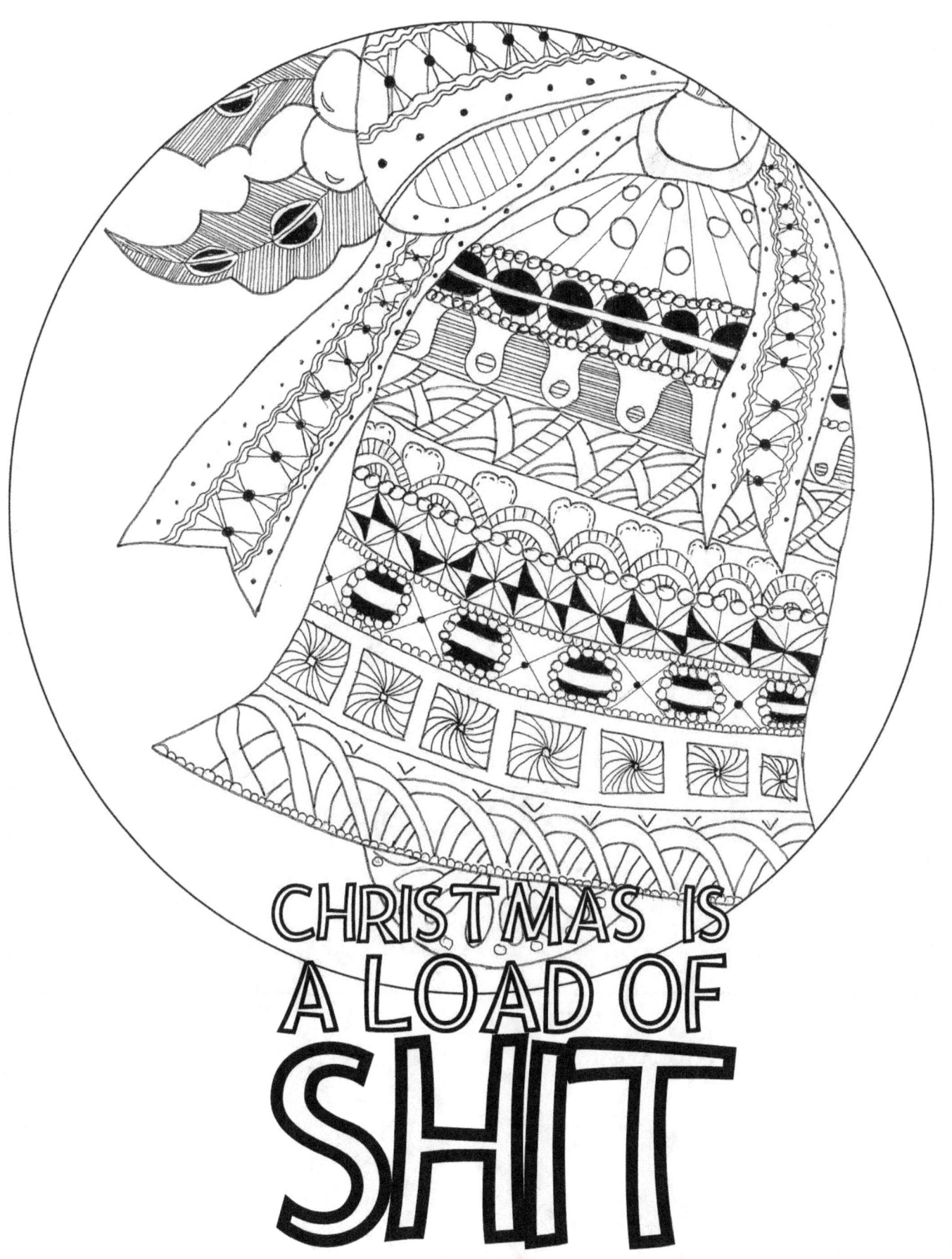

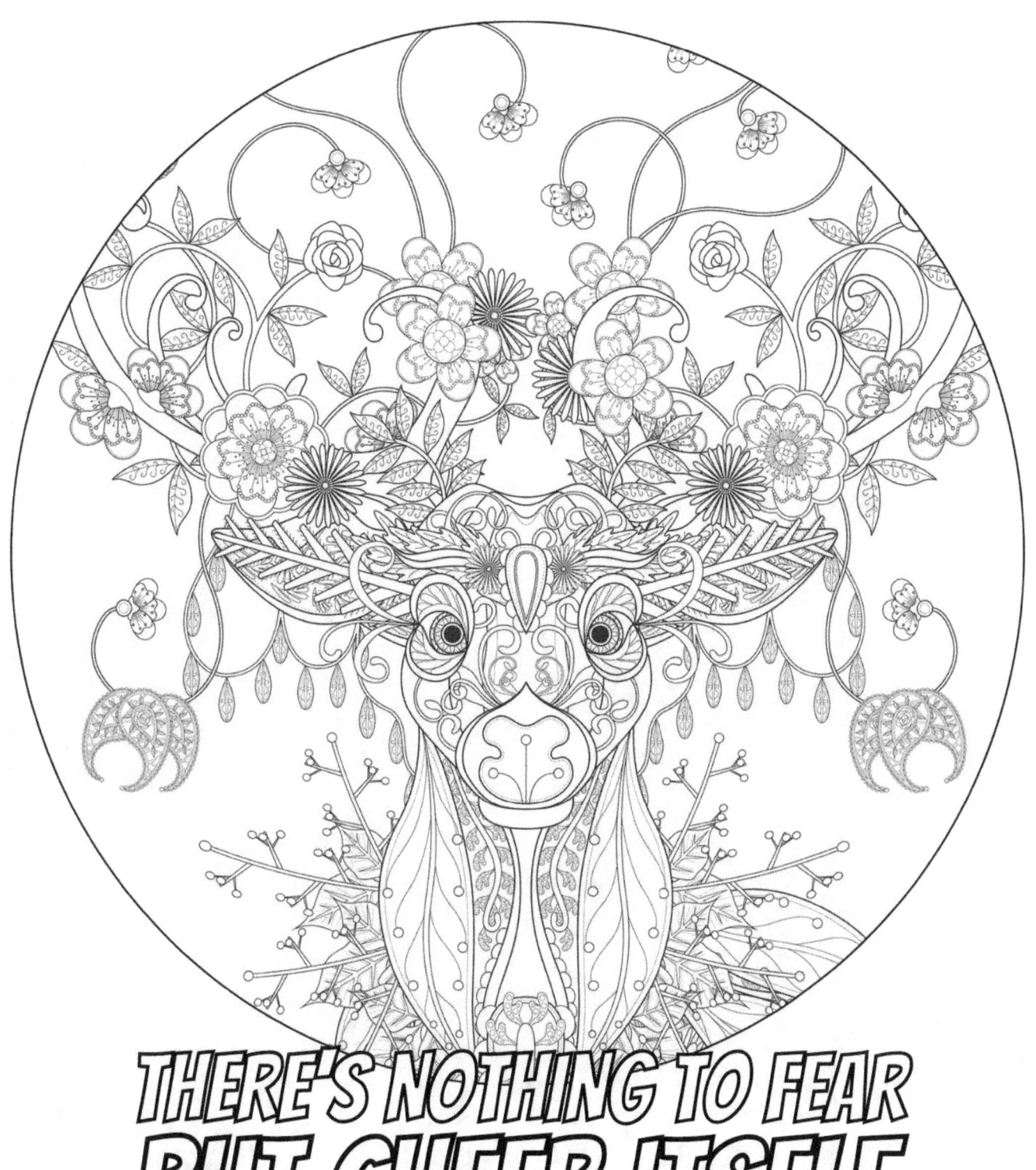

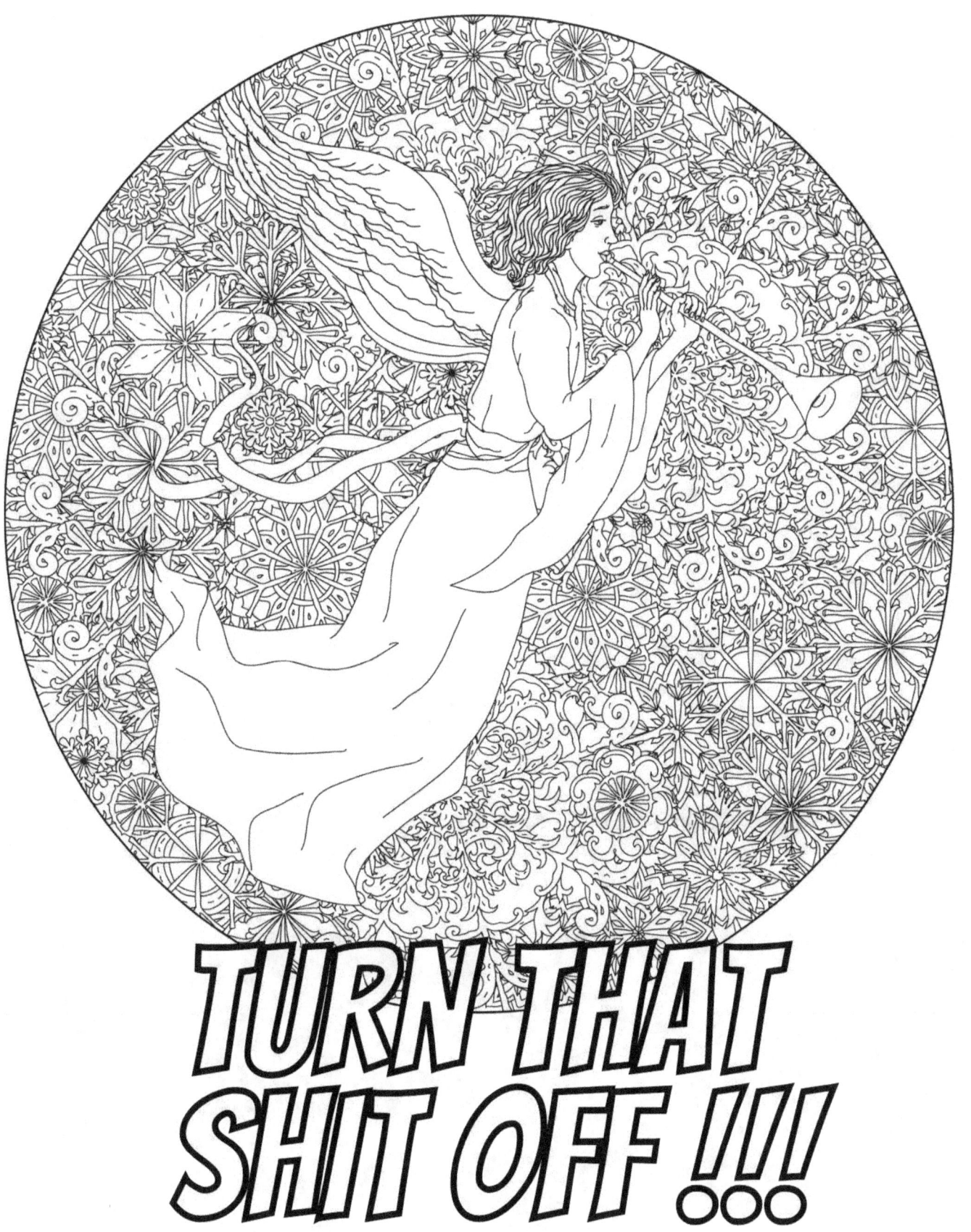

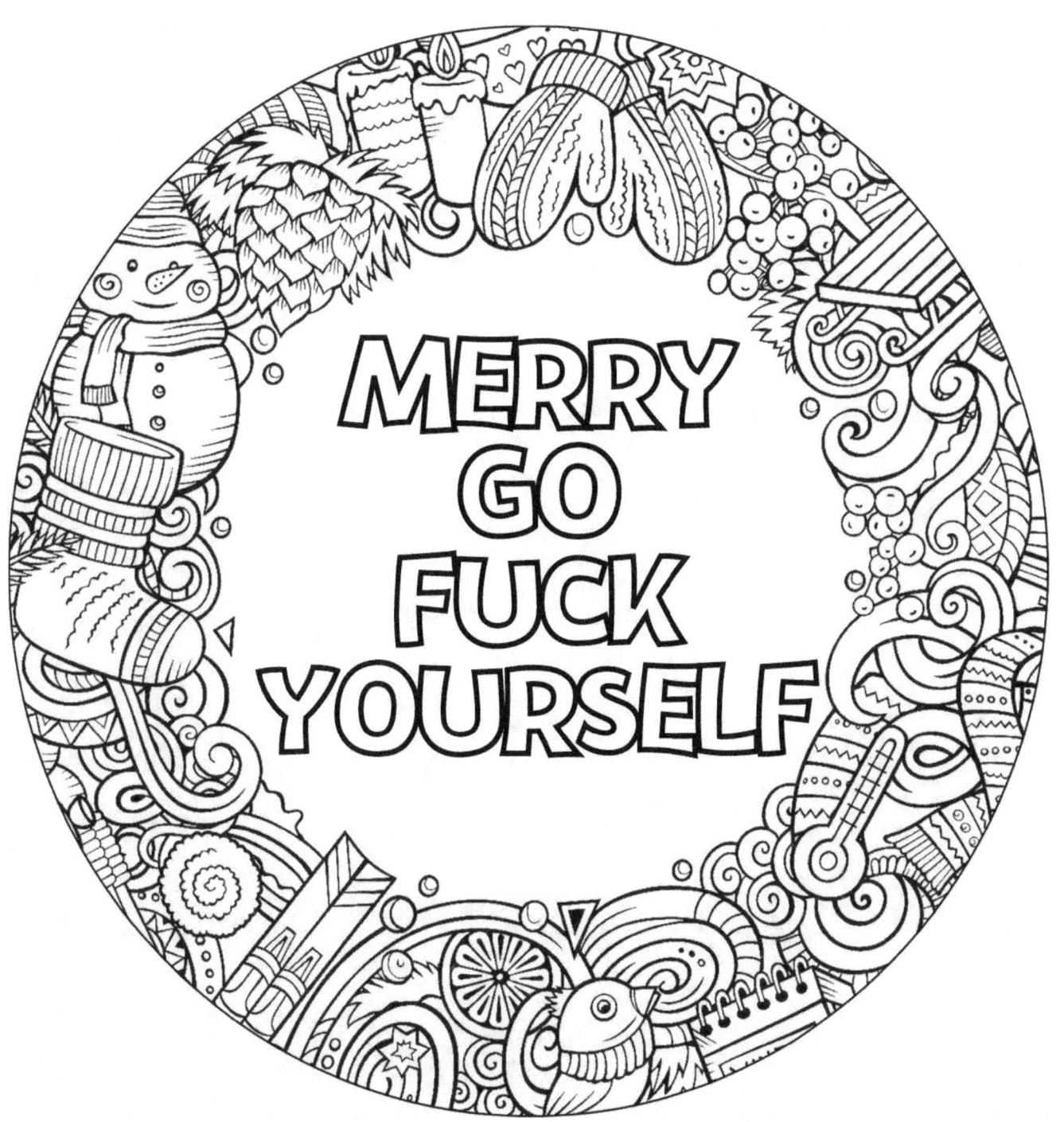

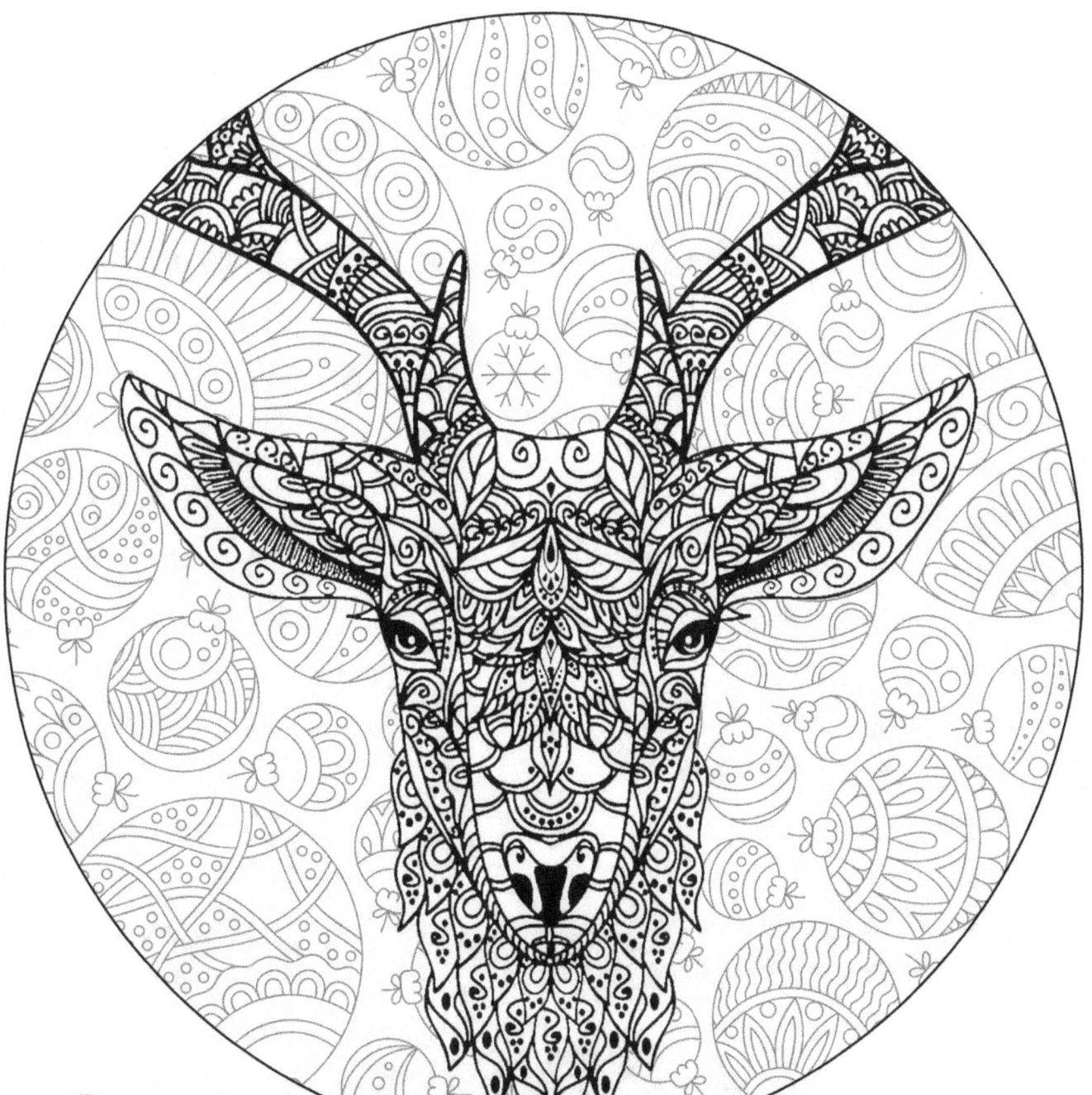

Dashing through the ......

NO!!!...

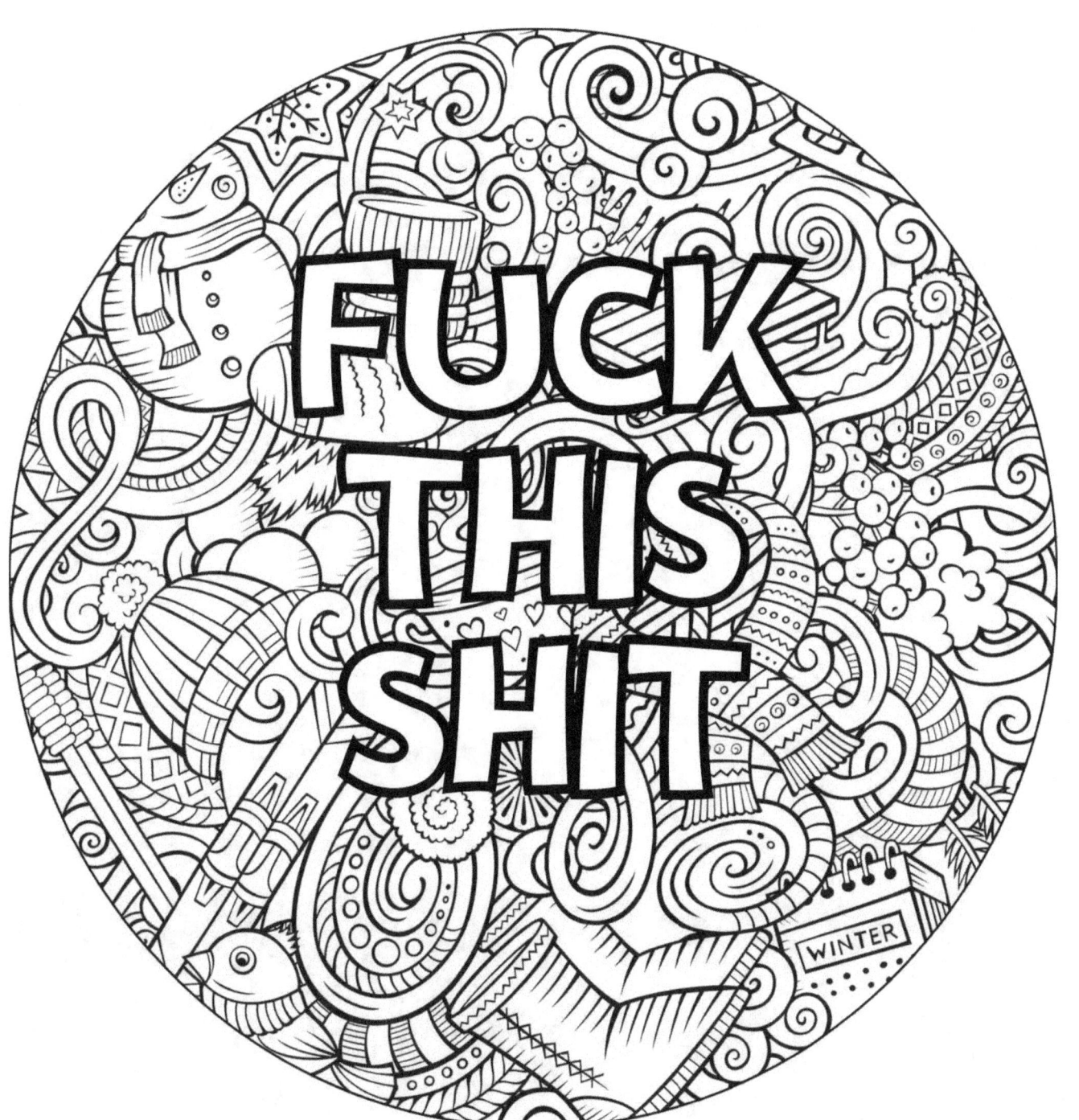

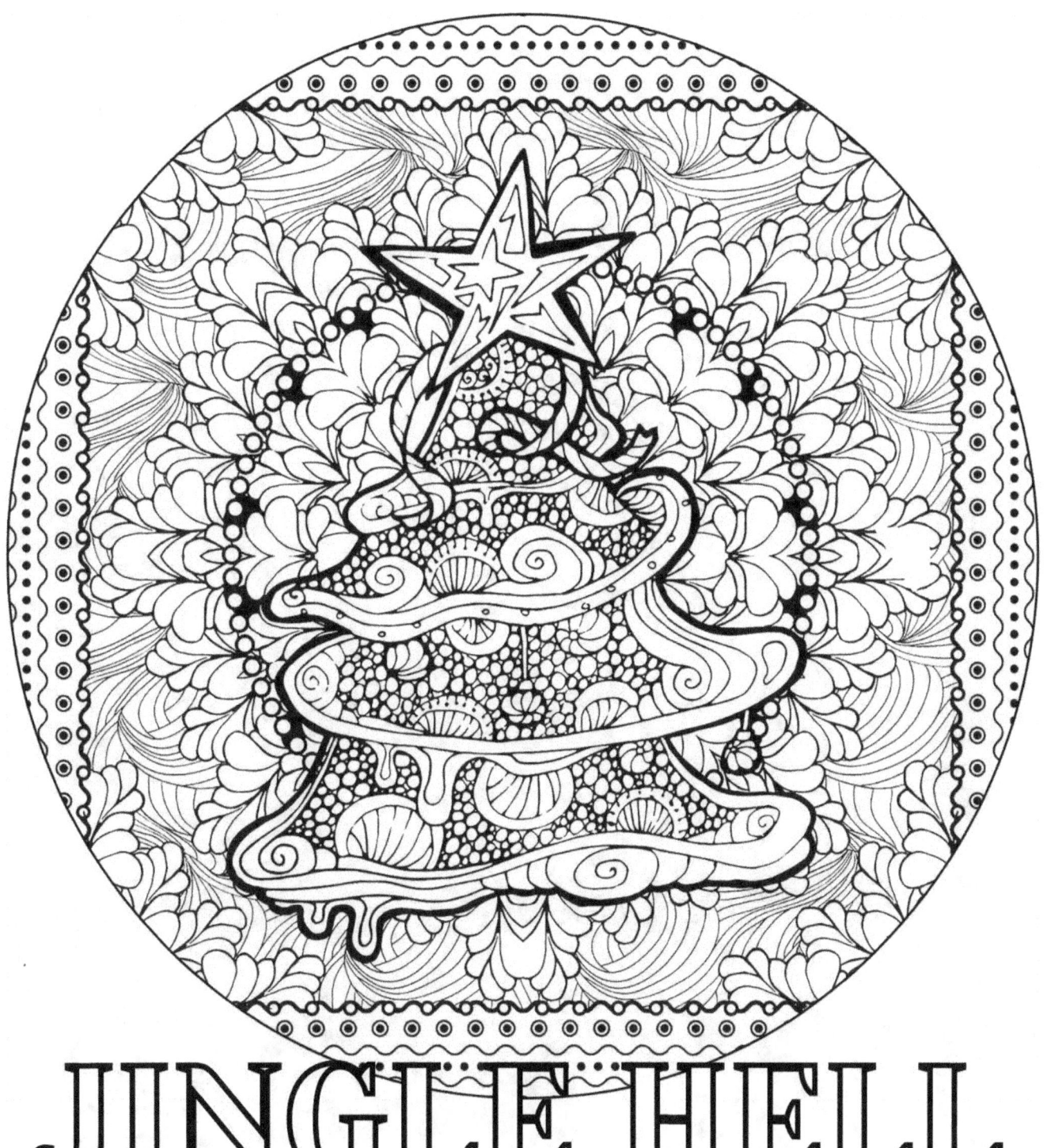

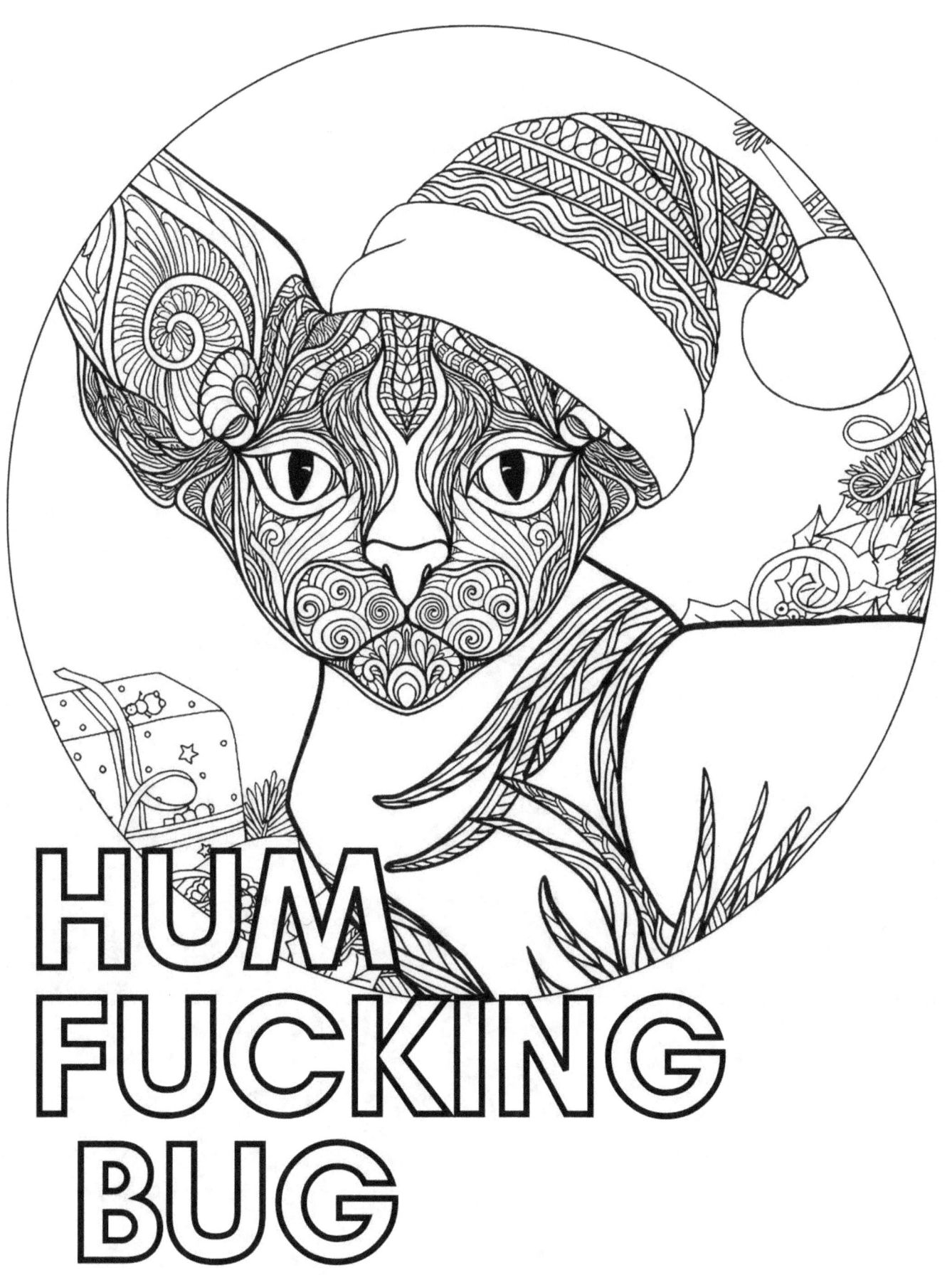

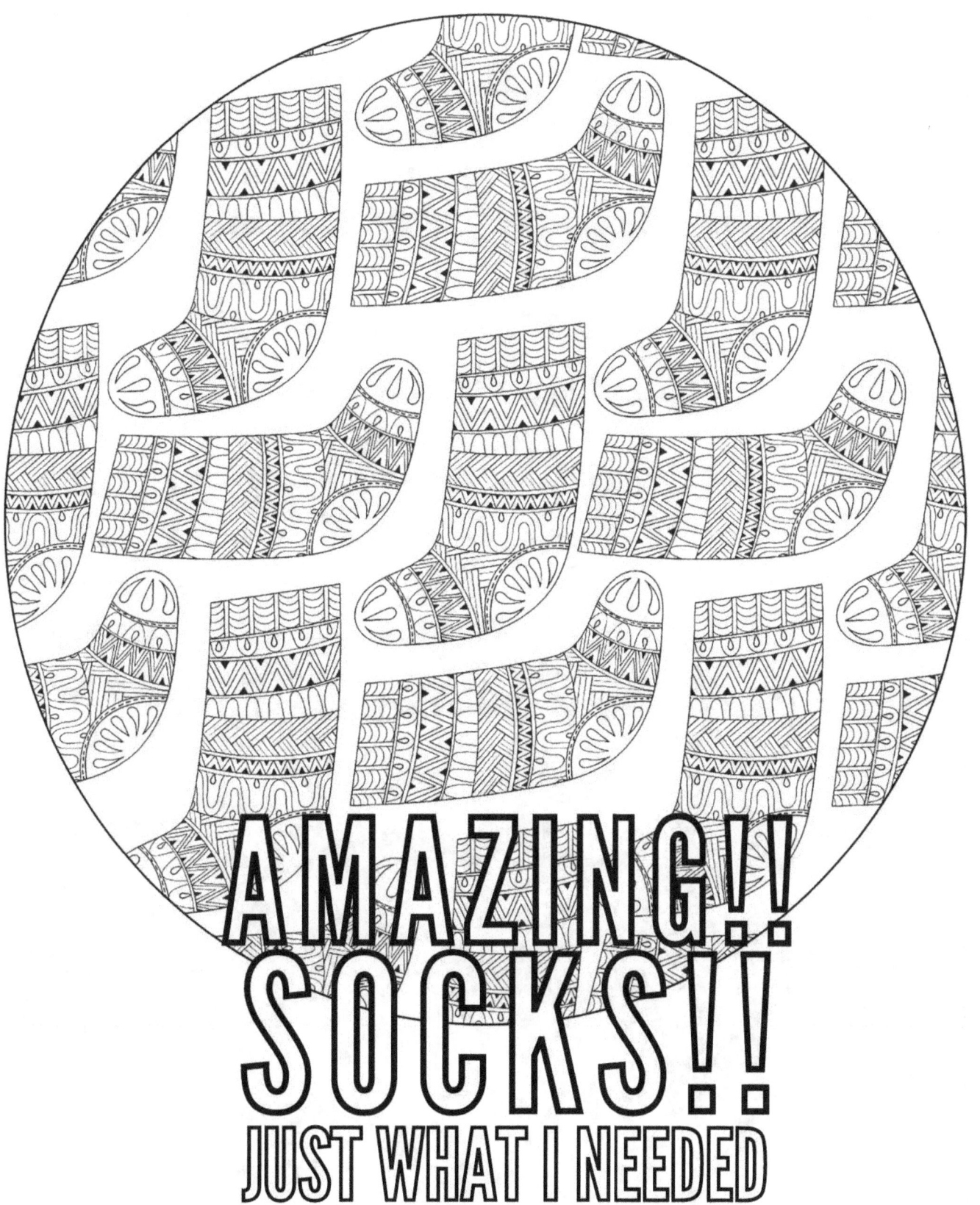

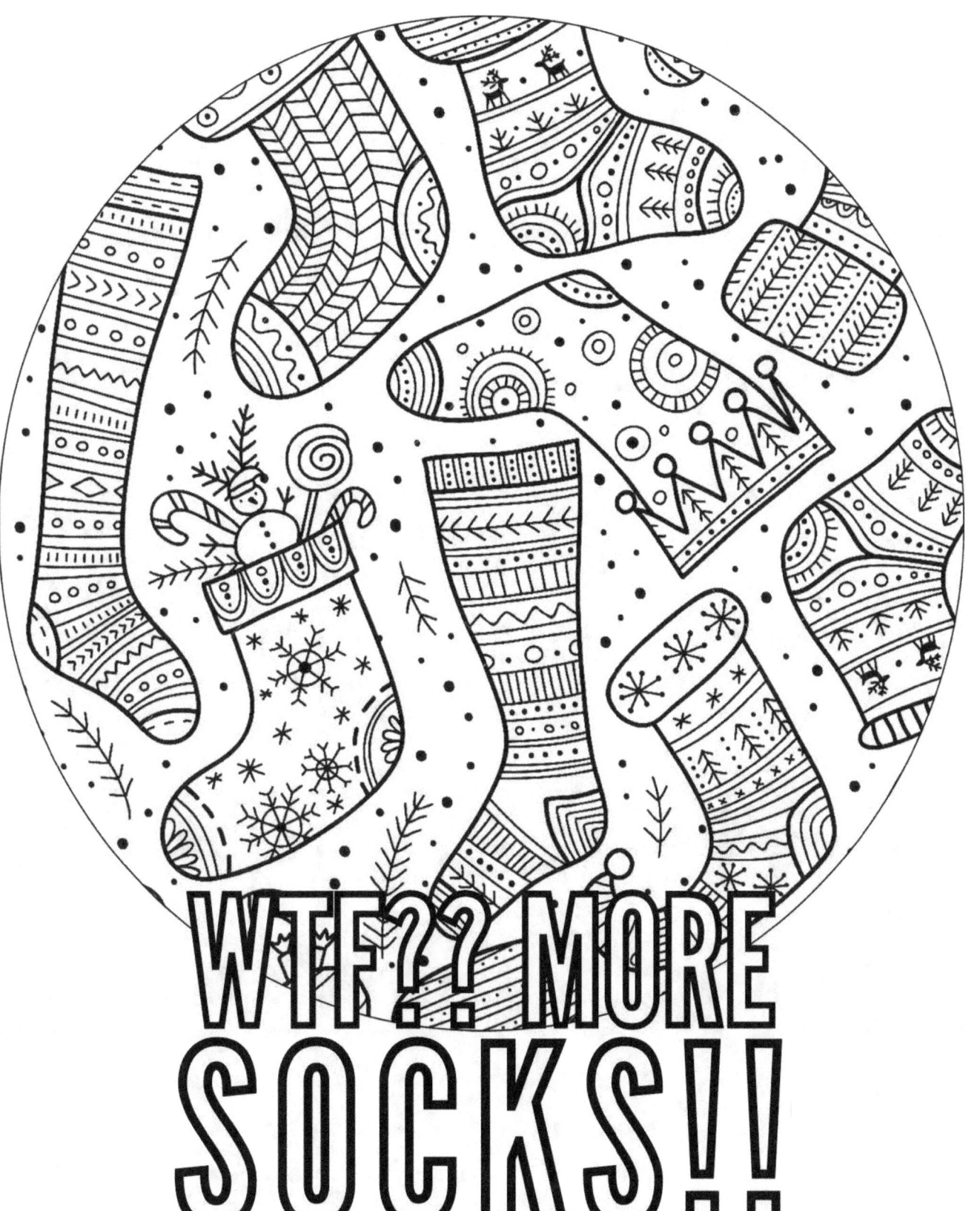

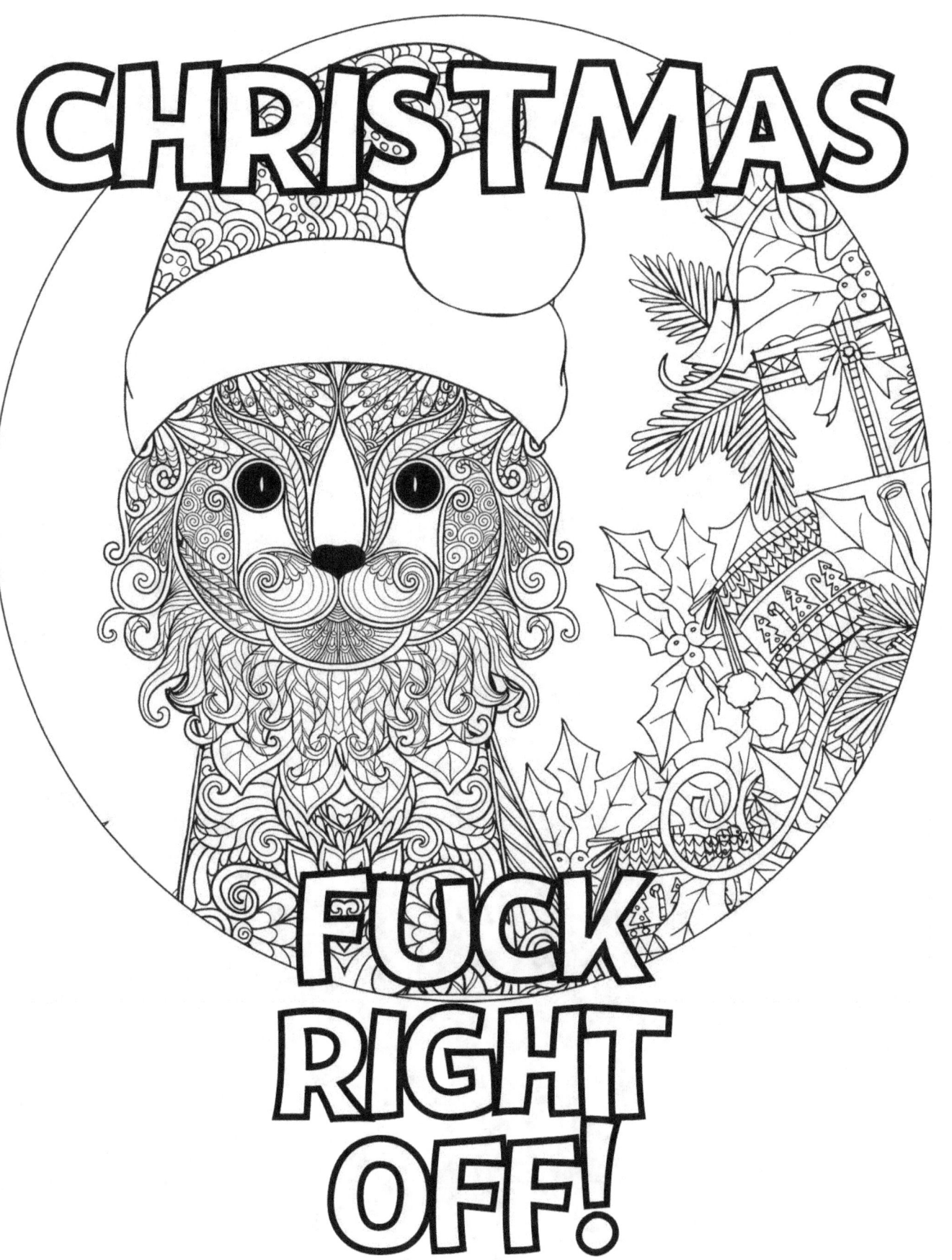

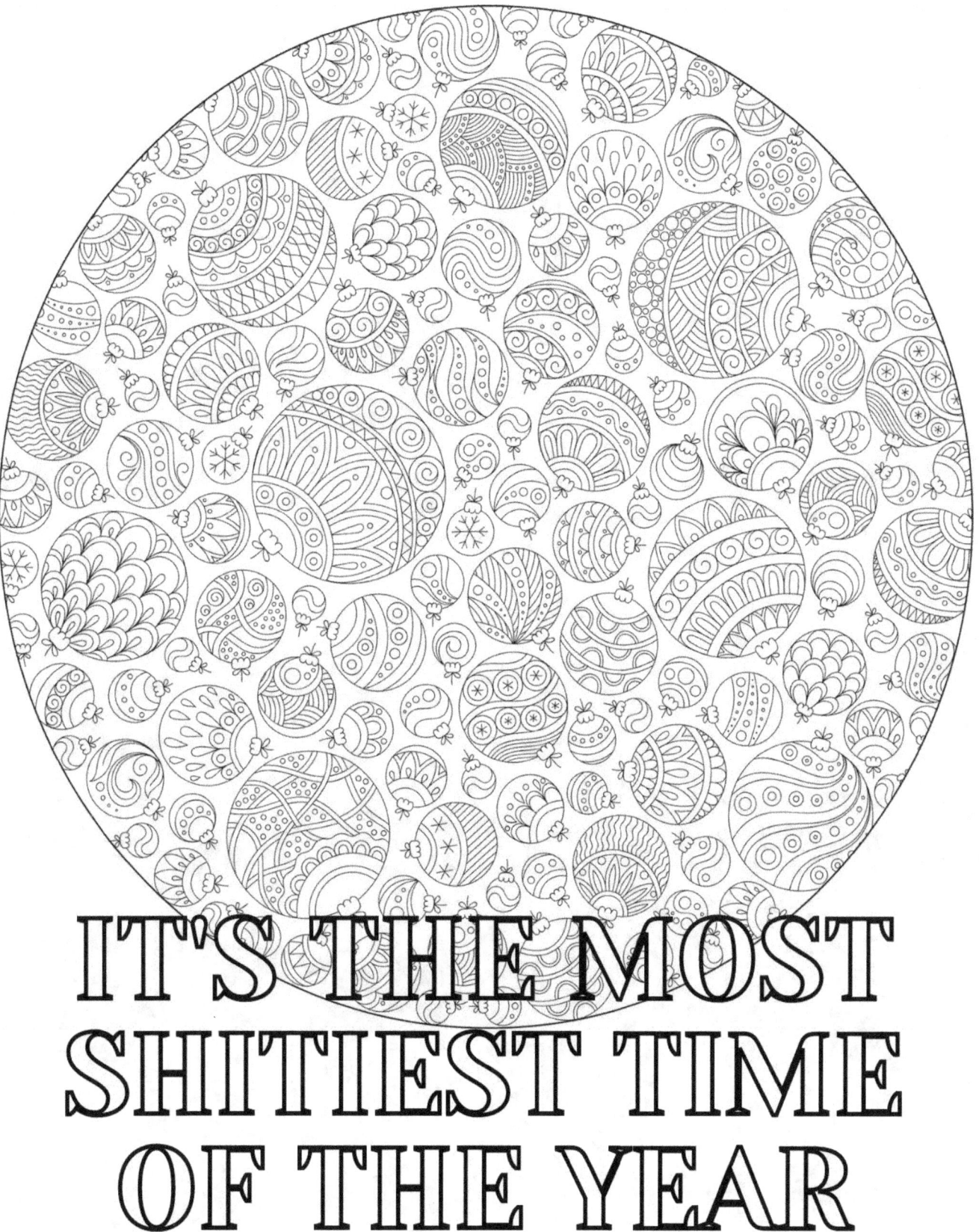

ANTI - CHRISTMAS

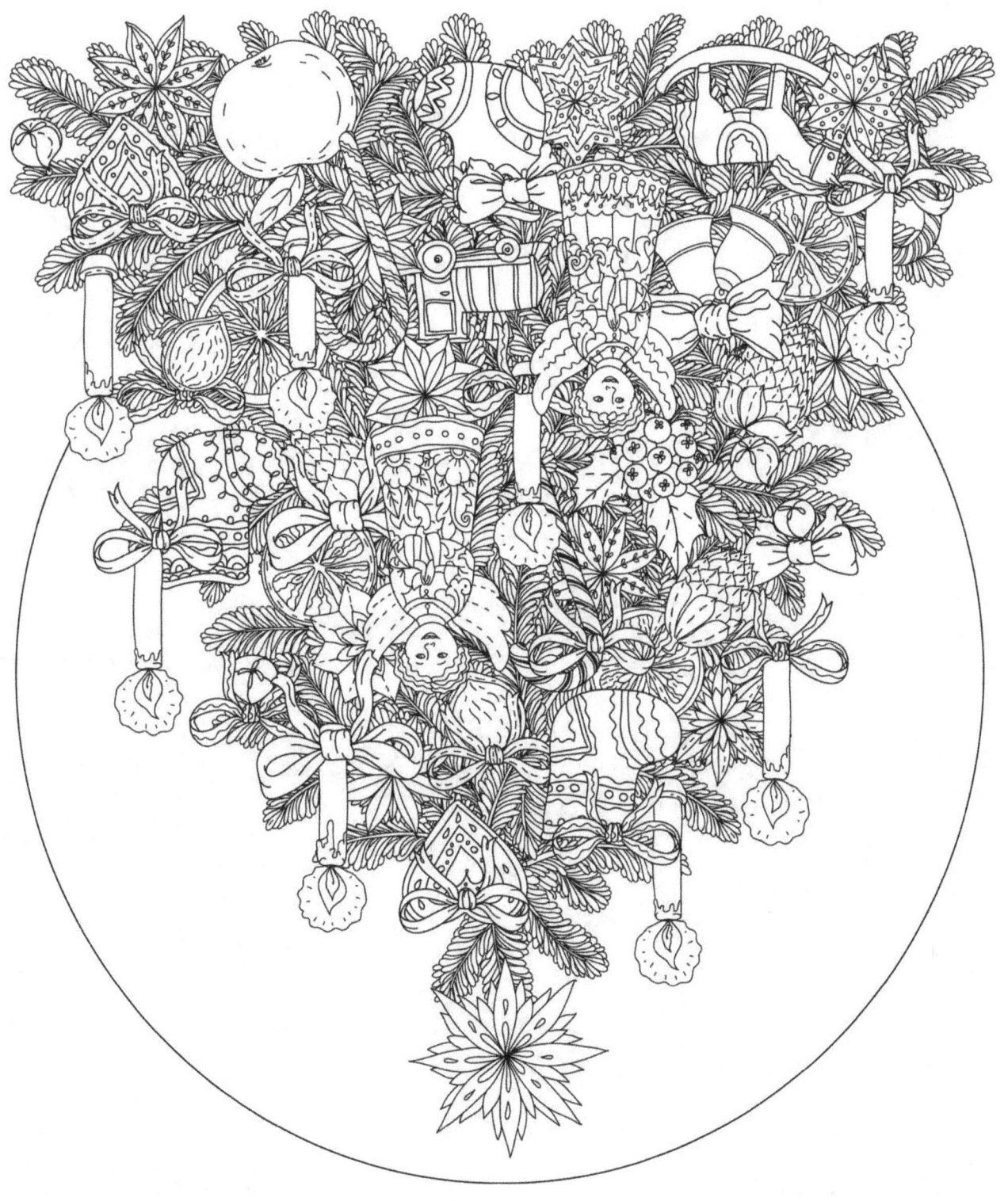

www.ingramcontent.com/pod-product-compliance
Lightning Source LLC
Chambersburg PA
CBHW081708220526

45466CB00009B/2921